Edward Randall Knowles

The Supremacy of the Spiritual

Edward Randall Knowles

The Supremacy of the Spiritual

ISBN/EAN: 9783337334741

Printed in Europe, USA, Canada, Australia, Japan

Cover: Foto ©Lupo / pixelio.de

More available books at **www.hansebooks.com**

THE SUPREMACY

OF THE

SPIRITUAL.

———————

BY

EDWARD RANDALL KNOWLES,
LL. D.

THE SUPREMACY OF THE SPIRITUAL.

THE further and more logically scientists proceed with the question of the one only absolute reality, the closer they approach to the full acceptance of the conclusions which I have for years advocated concerning the absolute supremacy of the spiritual. A striking example of this is to be found in Doctor Thornton's "Philosophy of the Three Ethers." The first, which he identifies with Life, affords the potentialities of the other two.

All other theories call to their aid self-contradictory propositions, absurd ideas or vague theories, which would

need greater ingenuity to substantiate
them, even were they capable of proof,
than the clear and simple truth of the
One Substance, the only Life, Spirit and
Power in absolute existence.

"We feel but the pulse of that viewless Hand
    Which has ever been and still shall be,
In the stellar orb and the grain of sand,
    Through nature's endless paternity."

So much has been written, and so
ably, upon this subject, that I should be
indisposed to venture upon this field of
discussion were it not for the fact that
I may be able, in my imperfect way, to
offer some suggestions which are new
and original, and which, I am convinced,
are absolutely true and perfectly logical
and clear.

Scientists assume the being and
action of a substance, omnipresent
throughout infinite space, which com-

municates light, heat, electricity and gravitation from one body to another, and even mental emotion and imaginary ideas from one mind to another. This omnipresent medium they call "the ether," attributing to it, in the case of some phenomena, qualities utterly incompatible with those which they are compelled to assign to it in the examination of other phenomena. An omnipresent substance of some kind, however, is a necessary inference from the following facts : —

The planets attract each other, and are all attracted by the sun.

It is generally agreed that the atmosphere does not, in its most attenuated degree, extend more than three hundred miles beyond the earth's surface.

Heat, light, electricity, magnetism and gravitation operate in an exhausted receiver just as well as elsewhere.

One mind sometimes influences another independently of ordinary sensation or muscular motion, without contact or perceptible connection.

Says Professor Tyndall: " The domain in which this motion of light is carried on lies entirely beyond the reach of our senses. The waves of light require a medium for their formation and propagation, but we cannot see or feel or taste or smell this medium. How, then, has its existence been established? By showing that by the assumption of this wonderful intangible *ether* all the phenomena of optics are accounted for with a fulness and clearness and conclusiveness which leave no desire of the intellect unfulfilled. When the law of gravitation first suggested itself to the mind of Newton, what did he do? He set himself to examine whether it accounted for all the facts. He determined the courses of the planets ; he calculated the rapidity of the moon's fall toward the earth ; he considered the precession of the equinoxes, the ebb and flow of the tides, and found all explained by the law of gravitation. He, therefore, regarded this law as established, and the verdict of science subsequently confirmed his conciusion. On similar, and if possible, on stronger grounds, we found our belief in the existence of the universal ether. It explains facts far more various and complicated than those on which Newton based his law. If a single phenomenon could be pointed out which the ether is proved incompetent to explain, we should have to give it up ; but no such phenomenon has ever been pointed out. It is, therefore, at least as certain that space is filled with a medium by means of which suns

and stars diffuse their radiant power as
that it is traversed by that force which
holds, not only our planetary system,
but the immeasurable heavens them-
selves in its grasp."

Thus Professor Tyndall clearly and
conclusively proves the certainty of the
existence of an omnipresent substance
acting as the medium of many of the
phenomena of the universe. But in
doing so, he proves far more than he
probably ever intended to prove. While
the existence of this medium is clearly
proven, yet the most superficial consid-
eration of the phenomena of light, heat,
gravitation, electricity and magnetism
readily shows that it is necessary to assign to this medium in the case of some
phenomena qualities utterly incompatible, according to the laws of matter,
with its action in the case of other
phenomena, and hence that this medium

must be a substance which transcends the known laws of this material world. Furthermore, the hypothesis of one medium as the basis of light, for example, a different one for gravitation, and yet another for electricity, is wholly inadmissible, since it supposes two or more substances existing and operating in exactly the same point of space (an utter absurdity according to the laws of the material world alone) and without either one nullifying or excluding the action of the other, or others.

Admitting, therefore, the clearly proven existence of this "ether" (or whatever you may please to call it), it is yet necessary to proceed further and recognize the fact that this single universal medium is not only omnipresent, but immaterial, and hence not of the material existence and its condi-

tions and laws, but spiritual.   We find
it to be

> " A motion and a spirit that impels
> All thinking things, all objects of all thought,
> And rolls through all things."

And right here, we recall the fact,
by the way, that already many scientific
men have supposed this so-called "ether"
to be homogeneous with the immaterial,
simple substance, the soul.   And this
supposition is confirmed when we find
the same spiritual substance operating
as the medium of communication in the
already well-known phenomena of
thought transference and mental suggestion from one mind to another.
The idea that the will of man can
direct the operation of this medium is
perfectly consistent with the nature of
the will.   In the case of the electric
eel, we find an instance of the will

directing electricity in such a way as to paralyze the limbs of animals at a distance, and even to cause death; and we find the invisible and spiritual medium of communication in thought transference and mental suggestion easily directed by the human will.

But there is one more phenomenon, or rather class of phenomena, to be added to our *data* before ultimately determining, according to the canons of scientific investigation and verification expressed by Professor Tyndall, the exact character and nature of this omnipresent spiritual substance and medium,— the class of phenomena known as matter.

Knowing that the will of man can direct the operation of this medium in " telepathy " and mental suggestion to other minds, we readily infer by analogy what we find to be the only tenable theory of the nature of the existence of matter: viz., that the ideal theory is substantially correct, so far as it goes positively to account for facts, and that this principle of spirit governed by will underlies the phenomena of matter. " That which truly is, or essence," is the proper meaning of substance. *Substance* is " the ultimate point in analyzing the complex idea of any object. *Accident* denotes all those ideas which the analysis excludes as not belonging to the mere being or nature of the object." The substance, then, of all matter, is spirit. The accidents of any object are its peculiar modifications. The accidents of all material objects are constantly sustained and presented, for the contemplation of created spirits, by the Divine Will in accordance with fixed and permanent laws.

At any point in space such presentation is constantly governed by the

Divine Will in such a way that an object there situated has a real existence *there*, whether any one perceives it or not. It exists *there*, in a special sense, as an idea of the infinite and omnipresent God, whose ideas, in the form of material objects, are infinitely more real than any image or hallucination which we can impress, by suggestion, upon the minds of others, and whose influence in our hearts is a far more stirring emotional power than any which can be imparted by merely human will to the most susceptible person. An object situated at a certain point in space is presented to the contemplation of every spirit who happens to come into communication with that point in space, this presentation being governed by fixed laws, and any one who has already perceived a particular object knows that upon going again to the place where it is, the same object will be perceived by him.

The recognition of the sole absolute existence of one infinite, omnipresent, eternal spirit does not conflict with a belief in this spirit as a personal God, Who is above all human comprehension, Whose ways are not our ways, and in Whom we and all created things exist. Yet care should be taken against affirming the statement " God is all," in a sense that really so limits God as to ignore the fact that an Infinite Being may have personality and must have an infinite power of self-adaptation in any degree, and thus must be capable of assuming the closest personal relations with finite persons.

Sir Isaac Newton held that God by existing constitutes time and space, He being infinite and eternal. In Him, and consequently in them, all created persons and things (His ideas) exist. We have a clear and necessary intuitive knowledge of unlimited time and space through Him, the omniscient, omnipresent, Eternal One, in Whom we exist, and of Whom we are, and because space and time are necessary to our present conditions of existence.

Our perception, therefore, of real ideas or material objects is the result of the action of the Divine Will on our minds, and the Eternal Spirit constantly sustains and presents these real ideas for the contemplation of created spirits, but they also exist, furthermore, *out of* the created minds which perceive them. Bishop Berkeley erred on this point; viz., in his maintaining of real ideas or material objects that " their *esse* is *percipi*, nor is it possible they should have any existence out of the minds or thinking things which perceive them."

This theory does not merge the creature in the Creator, as may readily be seen ; and, since it recognizes the free will and accountability of created spirits, does not make God the agent or power in everything that is done. Nor can it by any means lead any spiritually minded and clearly reasoning person to adopt Hume's view : viz., that the mind is but a mere series of impressions, and that we can have no knowledge of it.

Now, Berkeley erred in maintaining that the *esse* of things is *percipi ;* i. e., they can have no existence " out of the minds or thinking things which perceive them." He wrote, in the " Treatise Concerning the Principles of Human Knowledge " : —

" III. That neither our thoughts, nor passions, nor ideas formed by the imagination, exist without the mind, is what everybody will allow."

To this I readily agree, but not to what follows : —

" And it seems no less evident that the various sensations or ideas imprinted on the sense, however blended or combined together (that is, whatever objects they compose), cannot exist otherwise than in a mind perceiving them. I think an intuitive knowledge may be obtained of this by any one that shall attend to what is meant by the term *exist* when applied to sensible things. The table I write on, I say, exists, that is, I see and feel it ; and if I were out of my study I should say it existed, meaning thereby that if I was in my study I might perceive it, or that some other spirit does actually perceive it. There was an odor, that is, it was smelled ; there was a sound, that is to say, it was heard ; a color or figure, and it was perceived by sight or touch.

This is all I can understand by these and the like expressions. For as to what is said of the absolute existence of unthinking things without any relation to their being perceived, that seems perfectly unintelligible. Their *esse* is *percipi*, nor is it possible they should have any existence out of the minds or thinking things which perceive them."

The fallacy of Berkeley's reasoning is readily perceptible to us if we contemplate the omnipotence and omnipresence of the Infinite Eternal Spirit Who sustains the idea presented, as, e. g., a table. The very existence in the Infinite Mind of an object as directly and solely and especially related to a particular point in space, constitutes for it a real and special existence *there* (whether contemplated by any created spirit or not), without any relation to its being perceived by any other than the omnipresent Infinite Mind, its origin. Berkeley appears to have been lacking in an intuitive knowledge of the nature of the existence of the Infinite Divine Mind and Its power of thought.

Though our perception of real ideas or material objects is the result of the action of the Divine Will on our minds, and the Eternal Spirit constantly presents and sustains these real ideas for the contemplation of created spirits, yet their *esse* is not *percipi*, and they exist out of, as well as in, the created minds which perceive them. The table I write on exists; I see and feel it; and if I were out of my study, I should say it existed, but I mean thereby not only that " if I was in my study I might perceive it, or that some other spirit actually does perceive it," but that the table has an actual existence there, in that place,

whether any one is there to perceive it
or not.   This is because it is an idea of
the omnipotent and omnipresent Divine
Mind.

This theory, moreover, implies the
greater reality and the omnipresence of
the spiritual world.

Two worlds there are; the one is real,
  The other but seeming; both are *here*.
The seeming doth to us reveal
    Its attractions great and our friends most
        dear.

But greater far in the Spirit's light
  Are the pleasures of matter's sense bereft,
When the world of the seeming fades from
        sight,
    And the real existence alone is left.

And dearer yet our friends will be
  When illusions of earth from our lives have
        passed,
And the spirit from matter's bond is free,
  And the life eternal begun at last.

Prof. Tyndall, in his conclusive proof of the existence of an omnipresent substantial medium, yet remaining apparently content, and even desirous, to limit its conception to that of some material substance, reminds me of Saul of Tarsus, overwhelmed by the sudden light and power of the Eternal Spirit manifesting Itself in the personality of the Divine-human Jesus, yet feebly asking, "Who art Thou, Lord?" although he well knew that the God of Life alone could thus overwhelmingly subdue his stubborn spirit and manifest His own glory to Saul's mortal vision. And thus ever unsatisfactorily and inconsistently do scientists try to limit to the basis of matter and its laws the very underlying substance and basis of all material phenomena,— the Eternal Spirit and God of Life, who alone can sustain these phenomena which some of

His own little created spirits will persist in attributing to their "wonderful intangible ether."

" God of the earth, the sky, the sea!
  Maker of all above, below!
Creation moves and lives in Thee,
  Thy present life through all doth flow.

" Thy love is in the sunshine's glow,
  Thy life is in the quickening air;
When lightnings flash and storm winds blow,
  There is thy power; Thy law is there."

Now to sum up our theory and the question of its establishment. Spirit is the universal, omnipresent, substantial medium of all the phenomena of the universe and the underlying substance of all matter, constantly sustained in its accidents, for the contemplation of created spirits, by the Divine Will in accordance with fixed and permanent laws. All created things that exist are the ideas of God.

How have I shown this theory to be true? By showing that by its assumption all the phenomena of the universe " are accounted for with a fulness and clearness and conclusiveness which leave no desire of the intellect unfulfilled," neither any desire of the most spiritual heart. It accounts " for all the facts." It explains every possible, as well as every known, phenomenon. It may therefore be regarded " as established," and the verdict of all the past confirms it, as will all future revelation. It is founded on the strongest grounds. "If a single phenomenon," — to resume Professor Tyndall's nomenclature — " could be pointed out which " the foregoing theory " proved incompetent to explain, we should have to give it up ; but no such phenomenon has ever been pointed out."

" Thou, Lord, alone, art all thy children need,
　　And there is none beside;
From Thee the streams of blessedness proceed,
　　In Thee the blest abide,—
Fountain of life, and all-abounding grace,
Our source, our centre and our dwelling
　　place."

A clever and original but mistaken writer, whom I will here mention as Prof. X., and whom I find it expedient to quote as affording an excellent presentation of a bright explanation of electricity which, however, does not explain, writes:—

" There is, perhaps, no theory of electricity which seems rational and adequate to explain the mechanical effects secured by its use. Are these mechanical effects due to a transformation of mechanical energy into electrical energy at the dynamo, and the retransformation of electrical into mechanical energy at the motor? Or is the process mainly a *transmission* of mechanical energy from the dynamo to the motor? If the latter, the mechanical energy delivered by the electric motor has undergone no transformation since it was expended upon the dynamo."

Claiming that " electricity is mainly a method of transmitting mechanical energy," Prof. X. adds two propositions containing qualifications and conditions which render their effect in substantiating " a mechanical theory of the transmission of energy by means of electricity" entirely null. He thus states them : —

"*Proposition First :* — In a body which is a good conductor of electricity, the atoms, or molecules, may, by the expenditure of energy in a magnetic field, be made to rotate about axes which traverse these atoms or molecules, and this rotation may be communicated to adjacent atoms, or molecules, in such a way that lines of these elementary particles traversing the whole body may be set in rotation by a rotary motion suitably set up in these particles in one part of the body.

" *Proposition Second :* — While a conductor is being moved so as to cut the lines of force in a magnetic field, the atoms or molecules of the conductor are constantly magnetized, their magnetic axes being at right angles to the lines of force of the field."

Although Prof. X.'s first proposition is deliciously absurd as well as unnecessary, he probably has the idea that electricity is a means of transmission of energy and that every atom in an electrified conductor becomes a magnet influencing every adjacent atom, and so on at an inconceivably rapid rate of progress of influence.

Prof. X.'s propositions therefore amount to nothing more than a somewhat original, though not very difficult, series of applications of mechanical principles to well known facts in electrical science, but without submitting any tenable hypothesis or proving or discovering anything new concerning a true, rational, adequate and explicable theory of electricity.

Prof. X. concludes thus: "If this theory, by calling to its aid the ether of space, shall be made to explain the more subtle phenomena of electricity, it may place our theoretical knowledge of the subject on a parallel with our conceptions of heat. The necessity of such aid, is no more objection to the validity or truth of this theory than is the explanation of radiant heat by means of the ether, an objection to the dynamic theory of heat."

This is all true enough, but the fact is that the professor barely comes in sight at the extreme close of his argument of the principle necessary to be investigated for one to arrive at a true theory of electricity, and does not seem to have discovered it.

But I find that an expert electrician anonymously gives, in the *New Science Review* for October, 1894, an excellent anwer to the question, " What is electricity?" without going beyond the merely material phase of existence.   He says that "it is simply a form that energy may assume while undergoing transformation from the mechanical or the chemical form to the heat form, or the reverse."

This idea that electricity is a mode of transformation of energy retains the conceptions regarding energy and its source, nature, and modes of action, that are absolutely essential to be held to in order to obtain a true theory of electricity.

These conceptions are decidedly not retained, but, on the contrary, are entirely lost, by any idea of the *mechanical transmission* of energy by means of electricity. But all would be very different and intelligible were the expression " magnetic transmission of energy " to be used instead of " mechanical transmission." This nomenclature would not imply the absurdity of an essential atomic or molecular motion.

I believe that electricity, which may correctly be called a transformation of energy, is a constant series of magnetic inductions between centres of force, or " atoms," and is thus analogous to spiritual influence or to thought transference. Such magnetic inductions do not involve either atomic or molecular motion, and are similar to the conduction of an impression by a sensor nerve or the conduction of a volitional impulse by a motor nerve.

The force or influence first operating is identical with that transmitted, the very same and none other ; and a magnetic force may be communicated from one atom to another so as to coexist in both, one and the same force, without necessarily sustaining any diminution of its original power in the atom first in order.

In dealing with a force that is non-material we need not presume to apply a materialistic rule of conservation of energy nor to deny the possible multi-location of such a force — yet one and the same and entire in each location.

Here I must suggest that the most

correct statement possible concerning the conservation of energy is that the total " quantity " (as materialistic scientists say) of energy in existence is infinite. The non-dissipation of energy in the infinite continuance of magnetic inductions between centres of force, or " atoms," is shown by Lodge to be most reasonable. He says : " To all intents and purposes certainly atoms are infinitely elastic, and why should they not also be infinitely conducting ? Why should the dissipation of energy occur, in respect to an electric current circulating wholly inside an atom ? There is no reason why it should."

Electrical phenomena may cause, or be caused by, atomic or molecular motion ; but such motion cannot be shown to be essential to the power underlying electricity; which is the ultimate phenomenon of a partly ma-

terial character with which we have to
deal in passing from the material to the
spiritual. The force, power, or entity
which operates does not itself directly
cause any atomic or molecular motion ;
and the term " force " has been herein
used for lack of a more fitting name.
In the realm of the spiritual, the most
powerful influence is known to be the
most quiet and silent.

All the statements made concerning
the different origins of electric manifes-
tations have actually proved, by the
differences of conditions among the
several modes of origin related, that
atomic or molecular motion is only
incidental to the conduction of electricity and that the very reality of electricity is the conduction of ideas by the
immanent Power Who is present everywhere in His complete infinity. The
greater the intensity and the longer the

continuance of an idea imposed upon the universal medium of magnetism by the means generating such idea, or cause of electricity, the more potent will be the results.

The phenomena of magnetism, wherein a specific "force," or rather thought, known to exist at a certain point, is found to be also at the same time present at another point, afford the ultimate analogy which directs us to the knowledge of the nature of the material world, or of how the Eternal Spirit creates an idea, or object, and, under certain conditions and according to fixed laws, produces the same idea in some created spirit.

" Thou Life within my life, than self more
    near!
Thou veiléd Presence infinitely clear!
From all illusive shows of self I flee
To find my centre and my rest in Thee."

Ecce Regnum!

" My kingdom is not of this world."
"Behold, the kingdom of God is within you."

An earnest soul, in error's dread embrace,
Essayed this prayer: " Oh, grant me, Lord
　　the grace
To know the truth Thy wisdom doth impart,
And follow it.　Yet in my inmost heart
Thou knowest wilfulness and pride hold sway.
Unto Thy kingdom, teach me, Lord, the way."
To her the Saviour answered lovingly:
" Let not this world's allurements hinder thee.
'Tis in thine heart that heaven's blest king-
　　dom lies;
With me, uplifted there, thy soul itself will
　　rise;
And when the Christ thy faith and life confess,
Heaven's presence then thy very soul will
　　bless."

The Conversion of St. Augustine.

O Blessed One! Thy life,
   Incarnate once for me,
Now animates my soul,
   Enabling me to see
Satan's devices deep,
   And each alluring snare.
Call Thou my soul from sleep,
   Who dost all ill repair.

Around me float the clouds
   Of error, doubt, despair;
Extend Thy mercy, Lord!
   Destroy me not, — forbear!
But suffer me to live,
   Thy servant, Lord, to be.
Father! Thy Spirit give
   To raise and quicken me.

Blest Mother of my Lord!
   Entreat of Thy dear Son
That by this humble hand
   His bidding may be done.

O Saviour!   Let not pride
  Control nor hinder me.
Forever at my side
  Deign Thou, my God, to be!

The Conversion of St. Augustine.

O Jesu!   Tuus spiritus,
Pro me incarnatus antea,
Collustrat meam animam
Ut inferorum videam
Consilia et insidias.
E somno meam animam
Tu, Reparator, suscita!

Exspes mens mea æstuat.
Errores me obnubilant.
Per dubitationem da,
Domine, mihi veniam!
Parce, ut tibi serviam!
Sustine me et anima,
Pater, per Sanctum Spiritum!

Præclara Mater Domini!
Tuum precare Filium
Ut manu mea humili
Fiat voluntas Domini.
Ne regat me superbia.
A fastu, Jesu, libera!
Et me æternum adjuva!

The Day is at Hand.

Through the long vigil of the night,
To greet the dawning of the light,
I wait in peace, 'mid silence deep,
By expectation held from sleep.
>   *Sustine me, Domine!*

Though dark and endless seems the gloom,
Like to the quiet of the tomb,
I wait contented without fear;
The glory of the dawn is near.
>   *Judica me, Domine!*

The day is coming; Glorious Sun
Of Righteousness!   Thy will be done!
Throughout the vast eternity
Thy radiance shines triumphantly.
>   *Gloria tibi, Domine!*

Rest and Peace !

(A Thanksgiving after a Mission.)

Jesu! Creator! God Omnipotent!
To Thee in grateful praise each knee is bent;
Powerless are banished evils to molest.
Oh, dwell forever with us, our Eternal *Rest!*

Sweet Jesus! Resting calm in Thy embrace,
We know that Thou dost every sin efface;
And in Thy loving arms all sorrows cease.
Thou art our Rest, our Joy, our Life, our
    Peace!

The Love and Joy of Heaven.

I love Thy labor, Blessed Lord!
  Thy love is life to me;
And in the fulness of Thy grace
  A heaven of rest I see.

The rest Thou givest to Thine own
  Is not that carnal ease
Indulged by those who idly seek
  Their own poor selves to please.

It is a rest of perfect joy,
  The joy of labor given
The poor and sick for love of Thee,
  Which brings foretaste of heaven.

This little glimpse Thou givest now
  Of Thy blest heaven above,
Incites me here to strive to gain
  That heaven of perfect love.

And what does perfect love bestow
  But perfect peace and rest;

And countless joys bestowed by Thee,
  Who knowest what is best?

Jesus!   Sweet Saviour!   Grant to me
  This perfect joy to know!
In Thee alone that joy I find;
  Dear Lord, I love Thee so!

The Most Perfect Thing in the World.

THE PRACTICE OF THE PRESENCE
OF GOD.

" I live; yet not I, but Christ liveth in me." — *St Paul.*
"That which is not God is nothing to me." — *St. Teresa.*

My God! Who ever art
   Unchangingly to me
My All in All! My life
   Eternal is in Thee!

My Father! to Thy Will
   I helpless, trustful, cling;
In Thine all bounteous Love
   Forgetting everything.

My Jesus! Sweetest Name,
   All other names above!
My King! no boon I crave —
   No blessing — save Thy Love.

My Friend! of friends most true,
   Whose Love is infinite!
Grant that, forever, I
   May in Thy Love delight.

My Priest!   Who searchest all,
  To Whom each thought is known;
A mercy-seat of penance, make
  Each inmost heart Thy throne.

My Life!   My being, Thou!
  My life is only Thine;
For me there is no death
  If only Thou art mine.

My Heaven!   All else is naught
  Beside Thy Presence Sweet.
My Life in Thine, Thy Life in mine —
  Make thus my soul complete.

Ad Reginam.

Thou who, of all on earth,
  Art to my soul most dear!
Each moment's consciousness
  Reveals thy presence here.
Nor space nor time can change
  This bond of sympathy;
Naught can our souls estrange
  In their firm constancy.

My Queen! Thy faithful heart
  Calls me with eloquence;
Where'er on earth thou art,
  My spirit hastens thence.
With equal loyalty
  My burning love insists;
Though I am far from thee,
  Thy life in mine exists.

My own! Fate's tyranny
  Now seems to bow us down,
And blighting care alone
  Appears our love to crown.

Yet, in the future, dawns
  A day of joy and peace;
The Power that blest our love
  Will give us sure release.

Our very life and love
  Declare a certainty
That over every chance
  Triumphant they will be.
The life that gave them birth
  Maketh our spirits one.
My Love! No power of earth
  Can sever us — mine Own!

True Catholicism.

You ask me why I am a Catholic.
  I've tried to answer you in prose, in vain.
From giving you a tedious, lengthy argument
  (The story is a long one) I refrain.

I am a Catholic because my heart
  Yearns to extend its fellowship to all
Who claim the sacred name of Christian, and
    my mind
  Finds no discrimination in the Master's call

To make one fold under one Shepherd's care
  And unity's most vital bond maintain;
Professing everywhere alike one common
    faith,
  Acknowledging one universal Head to
    reign.

Holy and apostolic is that rule
  Which doth the wondrous Son of God con-
    fess,
Keeping our holy faith in its integrity,
  Extending now its universal reign to bless

All nations and all lands, throughout the
    earth,
  Beneath its sway of spiritual power,
Which has its origin and strength in thee, O
    Christ!
  Of yesterday, to-day, the same forevermore!

Hymn to St. Aloysius.

O Saint of Beauty! on whose princely brow
  There rests a crown of peerless innocence,
Thy loving children come before thee now,
  Thy prayers entreating for their souls' de-
    fence.

Help of the Orphans! unto Jesus blest
  Offer their sufferings, piteous tears and
    woes.
His love alone brings sweet relief and rest;
  His peace will give their aching hearts re-
    pose.

O noble Youth! child of the Sacred Heart!
  Whom Jesus loved so dearly as to deign
His boundless grace unto thy soul impart,
  Choosing thee endlessly to share His reign.

Patron of Youth! implore faith's guiding light
  To lead our souls on to heaven's portal
    high,
Till, in the dawn from purgatorial night,
  Into thine outstretched, welcoming arms
    we fly.

St. Thomas the Apostle.

DECEMBER 21, 1891.

While doubts that from our human frailty rise
  Oft hinder us and thrust us far from Thee,
Yet honest doubt that in the pathway lies
  Of those who love Thee and are wholly free
To plead Thy cause and fight Thy battle well,
  Who yet for Thee would urge a flawless
    plea
And most convincingly Thy gospel tell,
  May draw them even nearer yet to Thee.
To such confirm, dear Lord, their joyous faith,
  Strength the love that caused it, and inspire
Wisdom and zeal, and faithfulness till death.
  Bid doubt and error from their minds re-
    tire,
And when their hearts by fears and griefs
    are torn,
  Make them, dear Lord, amidst the strife
    recall
With love the wounds Thy Sacred Heart has
    borne,
  And know in Thee their Lord, their God,
    their All!

Conversion of St. Paul the Apostle.

As o'er the road of life we erring go,
  Oft, in the fainting spirit's darkest hour,
Heaven's inspiration shineth round about,
  O'erwhelming us with sudden truth and
  power.

" Who art Thou, Lord? " at once we feebly
  ask,
Although full well we know the God of Life
Alone our dying spirits thus can rouse,
  Against Whose Will we waged a futile
  strife.

" What wilt Thou have me, Lord, to do? "
  Trembling, astonished, overcome, we ask;
Repentant, looking upward eagerly,
  We seek some heaven-appointed task.

Let us, obedient, Heaven's light implore,
  And follow it, however rough our road,
With patient faith, for thus alone we gain
  The way to Truth, to Life, to Peace, to God.

Personal Reflections.

[On Presenting a Mirror to a Lady.]

This mirror, framed 'mid ancient carvings
    rare,
  Which hath for centuries the charms por-
    trayed
Of distant Persia's noblest ladies fair
  In splendors oriental bright arrayed;
Destined to yet reflect a charming face,
  Of calm repose and with expression sweet,
Reigning above a form of matchless grace;
  O Lady fair, with worthy charms replete!
    This souvenir I give to thee,
    Thus to fulfil its destiny.

The Rule of St. Benedict.

O Benedict! thrice bless*é*d thou,
    In life as well as name.
The value of thy holy zeal
    Earth's utmost bounds proclaim.

To teach our blest Redeemer's love,
    To keep alive His praise,
In time of need Heaven's mercy deigned
    Thy stalwart soul to raise.

" Whatever work of good to thee
    Sweet Jesus deigns to send,
Beg of Him with thine earnest prayer
    To guide it to the end."

Thus taught the good St. Benedict;
    And, through the ages long,
The Holy Ghost maintains for him
    His rule — Faith's bulwark strong.

Mater Gloriosissima.

Mater Gloriosissima!
Cum universo animo
Tibi aguntur gentibus
Honor et benedictio.

Jesu Voluntas Eadem,
Quæ ex Infantis pectore
Beatam tuebatur te,
Nunc omnia movet dicere.

Voluntas Dei Filii,
Omnipotens per omnia,
Decrevit revereri te
Pæne divina gloria.

Mater Gloriosissima.

Mother Most Glorious! Queen of Heaven! to
  thee
  With one consent all nations voice acclaim;
All generations, as forever, now
  Rev'rently hail thee, lauding thy sweet
  name.

The will that in the little Saviour's Heart
  Impelled His dawning human concious-
  ness,
An Infant claspéd in thy loving arms,
  Now doth impel all creatures thee to bless.

That mighty Will,—the Will of God's dear
  Son!
  Of God Himself—the glorious Trinity!—
Now moveth all things to ascribe to thee
  Every perfection save Divinity.

"Thy Kingdom Come."

"Thy kingdom come," vainly the people
    pray,
Closing their eyes to evils at their side,
Worshipping self alone, nor knowing where
    In very truth God's kingdom doth abide.

But change, O God! the stubborn hearts of
    men
    From blinding errors base, from unjust
    laws ;
Teach them that wrong will only vanish when
    They first correct and shun each evil cause.

Henry Ward Beecher.

Tumultuous rage the wintry blasts without
My study window, as I sit and think
Of my environment upon the brow
Of this bleak eminence, where the drifting
    snow,
Wrapt like a cope about the mighty bulk
Of Sutton's tallest hill, a vestment white
Bedecked with icy gems, transplendent shines
As if on giant statue of some priestly form
Which 'neath heaven's dome of vastness in-
    finite
Kind Nature had, with foresight wonderful,
To mark the advent, work and memory
Of one at once her son, her friend, her
    priest,
With fond design anticipating reared.
(For Sutton knew him well, a kinsman dear
By fondest ties to her forever bound.)
E'en so, around great Beecher's bright career,
Raged with tumultuous fury bitter strife
Of creeds, of classes, and of partisans,
And war of factions — aye! of nations too.

And thus, in grandeur, did his lofty soul,
Nobly preëminent with majesty,
O'ertower those sons of men whom kindly
    fate
Had made the leaders of their time and land.
Ornate with gems of brilliant thought, his
    mind
Shone forth transplendent like this stalwart
    hill
Snow-white in purity and loveliness,
Keeping that heavenly consciousness within
Unmoved by outward turmoil or the thrusts
Of calumny demoniac that sought
With futile spite a noble fame to mar.
Serenely onward doth his noble soul
Progress upon the journey infinite
Toward the eternal's inmost, holiest shrine.
Most happy they yet waiting here, to whom
The least participation is vouchsafed
In his great influence, which, pervading,
    thrills
Sphere upon sphere as ceaseless ages roll.

Reality.

"Truth is the reality of things." — BALMES.

Substance of truth, Reality!
Joining in confraternity
Hearts eager to uphold the right,
And fortified by virtue's might;

Deific power, Reality!
O'erruling error's tyranny,
Eternal in thy majesty,
Yet lowly in simplicity;

O faithful guide, Reality!
Teach us to bear prosperity,
And let no selfish pride nor care
Our spirits' waning sight impair.

True Mentor, stern Reality!
Strong to assuage adversity!
Thy rule true consolation gives,
With hope inspired thy subject lives.

Love's motive, sweet Reality!
Attachment without sympathy

Most vital is not love at all,
But passing fancy's feeble thrall.

O Heaven — most real Reality!
Thou all-sustaining Deity!
Though thou art present everywhere,
The true alone thy kingdom share.

Thou guide supreme, Reality!
Lead onward to felicity!
Truth's life and power eternally,
Infallible Reality!

Meditation of St. Catharine of Sienna.

" Thou wert sad and in suffering because I was *hidden* in the midst of thy heart. Had I been absent, evil thoughts would have penetrated thy heart and have filled thee with joy; but my presence rendered them insupportable to thee; thou didst wish to repel them because thou didst hold them in horror, and it was because thou didst not succeed that thou wert borne down with sadness. I acted in thy soul, I defended thee against thy enemy. Therefore, beloved child, it is not by thy virtue, but mine, that thou hast so generously combatted, and merited such an abundant grace; now I will visit thee oftener and more familiarly than ever."

— Jesus Christ to St. Catharine.

Ah! my Jesus! Thou dost know
Why I did bewail Thee so!
Clear His answer comes to me —
" Know that, in my love for thee,
I have caused this earthly cloud
Once again thy soul to shroud,
That the pain of loss so drear,
After thou hadst known me near,
Might thy soul forever keep
From the abyss of self so deep, —
That thy dread despair might call,
When the struggle should appall,
Thee to turn eternally

From the world's false vanity
To thy Saviour's presence bright,
God of Life and Light of Light.
Nothing can be nearer thee ;
Of my life thine own shall be ;
Of thy love burns mine the life.
Here is refuge from all strife ;
Now in vain will foes assail ;
'Gainst thee hells can ne'er prevail ;
Thou in Christ and Christ in thee —
Thus to reign eternally."

To the Sacred Heart.

O Heart of Jesus! sheltering refuge blest,
Wherein alone poor weary souls find rest!
O pitying love wherein all sorrows cease,
Effacing sin and giving lasting peace.

O Heart of Jesus! from whose ardent flame
A single spark effaced Magdala's shame,
And wooed sweet Mary back to Bethany,
Regaining faith and innocence from Thee.

O Heart of Jesus! sacred fount divine,
O'er which the eternal Sun's fair glories
     shine!
O source from which the precious blood
     poured forth,
Each saving drop of priceless, matchless
     worth!

O Heart of Jesus! Perfect! Infinite!
In whose sweet love all blessèd souls unite!
Embodiment of universal good,
Eternal One! Jehovah! Jesus! Lord!

O Heart of Jesus! Whence this love for
    Thee ?
No love have I — 'tis all Thy love for me;
No life have I — save from Thy Sacred
    Heart,
Which, finding me, did all this love impart.